Introduction

The Sugg's Creek Church was established in 1800 as a Presbyterian church. Many of its earliest members had just arrived from the York County, South Carolina area. A number of those same people now lie buried in the Sugg's Creek Cemetery.

In 1867, Richard Beard, a professor at Cumberland University, recalled that the people at Sugg's Creek "were a noble band of people the likes of which I never expect to see again in this world." The records they left behind indicate this to be true.

Soon after its organization, the Sugg's Creek Church began to feel the influence of the "Revival of 1800" which was then sweeping the country. With the organizing of the Cumberland Presbyterians on 4 February 1810 at the home of Samuel McAdow in Dickson County, Tennessee, the Sugg's Creek Congregation immediately placed itself under their care.

The Cumberland Presbytery held its 1812 meeting at Sugg's Creek. The Presbytery met there two years later for a second time. The third and final meeting to be held at Sugg's Creek was in 1819.

The second meeting proved to be one of the most memorable meetings in the history of Cumberland Presbyterianism. It ratified and adopted the Constitution and Confession of Faith of the Cumberland Presbyterian Church. Both remained in effect until they were revised at Princeton, Kentucky in 1829.

Sugg's Creek Church today is but a remnant of its former self. Yet, it remains a church with a glorious past. The period prior to 1858 saw at least fifty great camp meetings and an equal number of protracted meetings. Such giants of the Cumberland Presbyterian Church as Finis Ewing, John Barnett, Thomas Calhoun, Robert Donnell, William Barnett, George Donnell, Richard Beard, and James A. Drennan preached there. Eternity alone can know the good done by this congregation.

Thomas E. Partlow
Lebanon, Tennessee

Sugg's Creek Church Book

Transcribed
from the
Original Records
of
First Presbyterian Church
at
Sugg's Creek Meeting House

Compiled By:
Thomas Partlow

Southern Historical Press, Inc.
Greenville, South Carolina

Copyright 2022 by:
Southern Historical Press, Inc.

All rights reserved. No part of this publication may be
reproduced, stored in a retrieval system or transmitted
in any form or by any means without the
prior permission of the publisher.

SOUTHERN HISTORICAL PRESS, INC.
PO BOX 1267
Greenville, SC   29601

ISBN #0-89308-073-2

Printed in the United States of America

STATE OF TENNESSEE

WILSON COUNTY

September 13, 1834

SUGG'S CREEK CHURCH BOOK

Containing

A short account of the organization of the first Presbyterian Church at Sugg's Creek Meeting House with a brief notice of the origin of the Cumberland Presbyterian Church at this place. Also, a record of names, births, baptisms, marriages, communions, deaths, removals, and other necessary church records.

TRANSCRIBED FROM THE ORIGINAL RECORDS OF

FIRST PRESBYTERIAN CHURCH AT SUGG'S CREEK MEETING HOUSE

September 13, 1834

ELIJAH CURREY
Clerk of Session

FIRST PRESBYTERIAN CHURCH AT SUGG'S CREEK MEETING HOUSE

In the year eighteen hundred the Rev. Samuel Donnel of the Presbyterian Body first organized a church at Sugg's Creek Meeting house. Elders-- William Hannah, John Hannah, Hugh Telford, and Robert Smith------. Reverend Samuel Donnel continued his ministerial labours two years about the time a great revival of religion commenced in the neighbourhood. From this time the Rev. Donnel declined the Pastoral care of the Church at this place, from that time untill the year 1808 the Congregation was supplied with circuit preaching by Alexander Anderson, Samuel King, and others--------.

In the year 1808 David Foster (a Licentiate) took charge of the Congregation--------. In 1810 the Cumberland Presbyterians constituted and became a separate body from the Presbyterians, about this time the Reverend David Foster reorganized a church at Sugg's Creek Meeting House called Cumberland Presbyterians----- and continued his ministerial labours untill 1827 at which time he declined the Pastoral Charge of the Congregation------------. On the 20 day of April 1820 the Church of Sugg Creek elected James Law and James Drennan to the office of Ruling Elder and on Friday the 19 of May following they were ordained to this office-----------. Upon the 13 day of May 1826 the Church at Sugg's Creek elected Reuben Wood and Thomas Telford to the office of Ruling Elders and shortly after they were ordained--------.

The Sugg's Creek Congregation having made choice of the Reverend John Beard as their stated Pastor whereupon application was made to Nashville Presbytery (according to Discipline) that he should preach to them one Sabbath in each month. Their petition being granted he proceeded to take charge of the Congregation April 10, 1828.

By consent of the Session Reverend John Beard applied to the Nashville Presbytery for a discharge from his congregation at Sugg's Creek. Accordingly, it was granted on the 10 day of March 1837 (?31). After which time the Congregation was still supplied with the labours of Rev. John Beard, Rev. Gideon H. Law, and others.

On Saturday the 15 day of May 1841 the Church of Sugg's Creek elected Reuben M. Wood and William Woodrum to the office of Ruling Elders and Moses M. Currey Deacon all were ordained the following day by the Reverend John N. Roach.

The Sugg's Creek Congregation convened on the 14 day of October 1841 and elected Rev. John Beard to the Pastoral office of the Church and petitioned the Nashville Presbytery for his labours two Sabaths in each month which petition was granted on the 20 day of October 1841.

The Sugg's Creek Church applied to the Nashville Presbytery for the services of Rev. J. B. Jackson as pastor which was granted 1852.

By order of the Session

H. TELFORD, Clerk

January 19th 1854
Wilson County, Tennessee
At Sugg's Creek the Session convened at 11 o'clock A. M.
J. B. Jackson, Moderator
Elders: Thomas Telford, Robert Brown, M. M. Currey, and J. N. Cawthan. H. Telford officiated as clerk.

    The Reverend J. B. Jackson offered his resignation to the Session as pastor after some discussion the matter was postponed untill Spring. The Session resolved that each member ought to feel it their duty to submit to the regulations of our church government and observe the rules of Christian propriety. The Session appointed Thomas Telford, Rev. J. B. Jackson, and H. Telford a committee on the ch book.
    The Session adjourned to meet on Saturday before the 3rd sab. in next month in the afternoon.

                                        H. T., Clerk Pro tem

Adjourned by prayer.

At Sugg's Creek
February 18, 1854
    Two of Session convened and a quorum not being present adjourned untill third Saturday in March.

                                        H. TELFORD, Clerk

At Sugg's Creek
On the 27 of March
Constituted by Prayer

    The Session convened and on motion they petitioned the Nashville Presbytery to be released from the obligation between them and Rev. J. B. Jackson as pastor which was granted. Present Thomas Telford, J. N. Cawthon, M. M. Curry, R. Foster. Absent R. Brown.

                                      H. TELFORD, Clerk Pro tem

Closed by prayer.

At Sugg's Creek Church
April 22, 1854

    Thomas Telford, Elder, and Rev. H. Telford only present. Absent R. Foster, R. Brown, M. M. Currey, and J. N. Cawthon, Elders.

                                      H. TELFORD, Clerk Pro tem

    At three o'clock-----. Recessed untill third Saturday in May. Concluded by prayer.

January 20, 1860

    Granted or gave seven letters (to wit) E. H. Miers, G. W. Mier, C. A. Miers, Mary W. Telford, Julia Ann Winters, and F. M. Telford, and L. E. Telford.

                                 HUGH TELFORD

February 18, 1854
At Sugg's Creek

    After service, Reverend J. B. Jackson, Brother M. M. Currey, and H. Telford met and as a quorum was not present has recessed untill March 27th 54. Closed by prayer.

    An account of the various scenes through which the Church passed is a very desirable object and should be a matter of record for the rising generation in the world. Since my boyhood I know H. Telford nothing of a lack of faithful preaching upon to 1827 by the Reverend David Foster. Some of the greatest revivals of religion have been here and some of the (lonest) of dark and destructive coldness. One of the great revivals was in 1820. Reverend John Provine traveled the circuit a great time for the church. One night, Esther Rice Jun'r. professed and next year -21- or 22 at Fall Creek two other sisters and Betsy Rice also a great many others I cannot now name at Stoner's Creek in September 23. I embraced Christ as my Savior in Oct. 1836. There I was received by the Nashville Presbytery as a candidate for the holy ministry and in 1842 at Ewing C. Rutherford C. was set apart to the whole work of the ministry by the laying on of the hands of the Presbytery. My ministerial course has been one of trial and difficulty through poverty and want of education and in all that time I have been sacrificing my time and health for the good of my fellow men.

Whereas certain scandalous reports injurious to the cause of religion having been circulated upon Henry J. Binkly (viz fornification with his sister in law) therefore the Session of Sugg's Creek thought proper to send two elders to converse with him upon the subject. They obeyed the order and he confessed guilt which they reported to the Session. The Session then notified him to appear before them upon the 14th day of July 1835. He came forward and acknowledged his guilt. They then admonished, rebuked, and suspended him untill he give a satisfactory evidence of true repentance.

Members present Rev. John Beard, Reuben Wood, Elijah Currey, Thomas Telford, John Roach, and all of us which concured in the decision. July 14, 1833.

THOMAS TELFORD, Clerk Pro Tem

State of Tennessee
Wilson County
June 11, 1836

Whereas William Yandle, a member of Sugg's Creek Congregation being charged by comon fame of using immoral language and fighting upon the 28th day of April 1836 (previous to citation he was conversed with upon the subject by two members). Then being regularly cited to appear before the Session of said Congregation upon the 11 day of June to answer to said charges. Seven witnesses being somoned (viz. John H. Cawthon, Eli M. Bradford, Moses M. Currey, Eli Sinclair, Solomon Carter, Wilee McDerman, and James S. Yandel, Sr. The Session met on the above date at Sugg's Creek Meeting House. Members present were Rev. John Beard, Thomas Telford, A. Gwyn, and E. Currey. Constituted by prayer. The accused being ready for trial the Session proceeded. J. H. Cawthon deposeth and saith that William Yandel and J. J. Roach commenced quarreling about lifting together. Yandel dared him to collar him. Roach collared him. Yandel struk him and used the word dadburn you and give the lie and they fought. J. H. Cawthon, Eli M. Bradford deposeth and saith William Yandel accused Roach of taking advantage of a stick in lifting together. Roach said it was an accident. Yandel charged him a second time. Roach called him an infernal rascal and collared him and they fought. Eli M. Bradford.

Moses M. Currey deposeth and said that while Yandel and Roach was lifting together the stick sliped. Yandel charged Roach with it. Roach said it was an accident. Yandel said I know better. Roach said he knew better. Yandel gave him the lie. Roach called him a dadburned rascal and collared him. Yandel said don't collar me. Roach said you have been telling lies on me. Yandel said let him come. I am as good a man as him and they fought. M. M. Currey.

Eli Sinclair deposeth and said Yandel and Roach was lifting at a log together. Yandel charged Roach of taking the advantage. He charged him a second time and give him the lie. Roach went towards him. Yandel dared him to touch him and they fought. Eli Sinclair.

Solomon Carter deposeth and saith Yandel and Roach lifted together. Yandel said Roach took the advantage of him. Roach said he did not. Yandel gave him the lie. They made it at each other and they struck. We parted them. Yandel said let him come. I am not afraid of him and they fought. S. Carter.

Wilee McDermon deposeth and saith Yandel and Roach lifted together. Yandel charged him with taking the advantage of him. Roach denied. Yandel give him the lie and dared him to collar him again and they fought. Wilee McDermon.

James Yandel, Sr. deposeth and saith from some things that p) he thought a quarrel was coming on. Yandel and Roach lifted together. Yandel charged him with being unfair. Roach denied. They contradicted a second time. Yandel give Roach the lie. Roach collared him. Yandel steped off some distance and told him to come on and they fought. James Yandell.

The accused was requested to withdraw after a few minutes private conversation amongst the Session. The accused was called in and told by the Moderator that the Session had found him guilty of both charges against him and wished to know whether he felt sorry for his conduct. He said I feel sorry it happened on account of the church. When asked if he did feel sorry for giving the lie and the banter he said he did note and would fight when imposed on (or would to that amount) he was requested to withdraw again when the Session decided as follows. That William Yandel be excluded from church privileges untill he give signs of repentance and sorrow for his conduct. He was called in and told the Session's decision. He appeared obstinate and made use of such expressions as these, what tame a lion, you can't tame me. It was born in me and still persisted in expressing his justification. Then the Moderator was requested to publish the decision the next Sabbath. He has since been conversed with by a majority of the Session and they still think he is impenitent.

ELIJAH CURREY, Clerk

Signed by order of Session June 11, 1836.

Whereas William Yandel thought he had injustice on him by the Sugg's Creek Session appealed to the Nashville Presbytery in session at Stoner's Creek the 7 day of November 1836. There decision was as follows. William Yandel being suspended by the Session of Sugg's Creek for immoral conduct appealed to this Presbytery after mature deliberation by a unanimous vote the decision of said Session was ratified in his case.

William Yandel appeared before me and said he wanted a letter. He is now under censure. Confirmed by the Nashville Presbytery August 17th, 1858.

H. TELFORD, Clerk Pro tem

Whereas it being public that B. C. Brown, a member of Sugg's Creek Congregation, did upon the 5 day of March 1842 engage in fight with Needham Jones. The Session of said Congregation shortly after met and resolved to send a member to converse with him upon the subject. Accordingly, he went. Said Brown agreed to appear before the Session and acknowledged sorrow for his offence. He came forward upon the 22 day of May and expressed sorrow and penitence. The Session admonished him and restored him to church privilege again.

ELIJAH CURREY, Clerk

It being made publick that B. C. Brown, a member of the Cumberland Presbyterian Church at Sugg's Creek engaged in fight with Mr. Hilton. The Session of said Church summoned said Brown to appear before them upon the 7 day of September 1842. Also, three witnesses (viz) Thomas A. Puckett, G. Peach, and Thomas Osborn--------. Session, being convened, constituted by prayer. Reverend John Beard presiding--------. Thomas A. Puckett, being called upon and sworn, testafieth that Mr. Brown was siting at the shop of Drs. Osborn and Logue and that Mr. Hilton came up within a few feet of him and said how are you Mr. Eight Dollars and a Half and abused him concerning an old matter between him and Mrs. Jones and her son, Needham. Mr. Brown said that had better mind his own business. Mr. H. said that Mr. Brown was not too good to steal that any man that would do as he had done would steal. Mr. B. stated that he had tho't that he would have nothing to do with him. Mr. H. used very abusive language giving him the d__n_d lie frequently. Mr. B. arose and told him that he could not suffer such language to be heaped upon him and struck him with his fist------. Ques. by Mr. B. Did you see in me during the time of his abuse a disposition to wave the matter? Witness, I did all the time---------.

Mr. Peach, being sworn, testifyed that Mr. Brown was siting before the shop door of Drs. Osborn and Logue and that Mr. Hilton spoke to him and said how are you, Mr. Eight Dollars and a Half, dam you, giving he the d__n_d lie frequently and said that anybody that would treat a widow woman as he had done would steal. About this time Mr. B. told him that he had thought that he would have nothing to do with him but after Mr. H. had repeatedly give him the lie Mr. B. arose and said he could not stand it any longer and struck him. Question by the accused. Did you see in me a disposition to wave the matter? Witness, I did.

Question by the Session. Did Mr. B. give him any cause at that time for the abuse? Witness, he did not.

T. C. Osborn, being duley sworn, testifieth that Mr. Brown was siting before him office door in company with several gentlemen who were entirely peaceble. I was in my office at the time. Mr. Hilton came up and therefore did not see the approach, but heard Mr. Hilton in a loud voice accost Mr. Brown with how are you Mr. Eight Dollars and a Half to which Mr. B. made no answer. Mr. Hilton made several such attacks as this before Mr. Brown seamed disposed to resist. I then came to the door and heard Mr. B. remark to Mr. H. that he had tho't. he would not have anything more to do with him to which Mr. H. retorted in an angry and abusive manner. At which Mr. B. seamed to get offended and said he would not stand that and puled off his coast and prepared for combat. Mr. Hilton's abuse rested upon an old grudge. Mr. H. said that any person that would do as he had done would steal. I have never heard Mr. B. say anything in reference to the old grudge previous to this affray that was calculated to arouse an indignant feeling-------.

The Session are of opinion that Mr. Brown done rong in striking the first blow. They therefore admonished and rebuked him and restored him to church privileges.

ELIJAH CURREY, Clerk

Mary Jane Robertson was born August 12, 1833.

Thomas Jefferson Barber was born March 18,1838 (?58). Departed this life November 3, 1913.

John Drennan was born in Pennsylvania in 1740. Departed this life in Wilson County on January 19, 1816. First Probate Judge of York County, South Carolina. Children of John Drennan.
  Thomas S. Drennan.
  James Drennan.
  Ann Drennan. Mother of Thomas Partlow, born 1796; died 1849.
  Rachel Drennan.
  (?) Drennan who married John Arnold.
  William Drennan.
  Joseph Drennan.

Register

Names	Births	Baptisms
David Foster Pastor	May 4. 1780	Baptized
Ann Foster	Apl 10. 1780	Do
Children		
Robert Foster	July 4. 1807	Do
John Carson Foster	Nov 7 1809	Do
Wm Colhoon Foster	Nov 22. 1811	Do
Isabel Foster	Jany 28 1814	Do
Nancy Allen Foster	Jany 2 1817	Do
Elizabeth Ann Foster	Mar 7 1820	Do

Marriages	Communicants	Deaths	Removals
July 1 1806	In Communion		
	Do		Removed by Letter
	Do		Do

Names	Register Births	Baptisms
Hugh Telford Elder	Aug 20 1764	Baptized
Jane Telford		Do
Children		
Thos Telford	Nov 11 1786	Do
Robert Telford		Do
John Telford	Oct 12 1790	Do
Mary Telford	Mar 20 1793	Do
Elizabeth Telford		Do
Hugh A. Telford	Oct 27 1798	Do
Ann Telford	June 9 1805	Do

Register
Marriages Communion Deaths Removals

In Communion June 5 1833
           Do

           Do
           Do
           Do
           Do   May 30 1845 { Removed by Letter
                                    { Rec'd by Do

           Do
           Do   Removed by Letter

18   Register
        Names   Births   Baptisms

Hugh Telford { Second Marriage }
Jane Telford   May 13. 1777   Baptized
  Children
Samuel Telford   Apl 25. 1809   Do
Jane Telford   Nov 18 1810   Do
Tirzah Telford   Feb 10 1815   Do
Washington Telford Jany 15 1823   Do

Hugh Telford { Third Marriage }
Sarah Telford.   Do

Robert Telford   Baptized
Nancy Telford   Apl 7 1791   Do
  Children
Thos. C Telford   Feby 1 1815   Do
Elizabeth Telford   June 6 1816   Do

16

Marriages	Communions	Deaths	Removals
[Jan?] 1808			
	In communion		
	Do		
	Do		Removd by letter
	Do		Removd by letter
	Do		

1813	In communion		
	Do		Removd by letter

Register

19 Names	Births	Baptisms
Benjamin Dobson	Aug 19. 1769	Baptized
Elizabeth Dobson	June 20 1774	Do
Children		
Elizabeth Dobson	Oct. 27 1800	Do
Wm. R. Dobson	Apl. 20 1803	Do
Jane Dobson	July 24 1805	Do
Margaret Dobson	Dec 31 1807	Do
Benjamin Dobson	Dec 1. 1812	Do
Ignathous Jones	—	Baptized
Wineford Jones	—	Do

Marriages	Communions	Deaths	Removals
Jan 27 1800	In communion		
	Do	Sept 27 1828	
	Do		
	Do		

In Communion July 7 1824
Do

Names	Births	Baptisms
John Roach Sr.	June 15 1769	Baptize
Rachel Roach	June 22 1770	Do
Children		
Wm Roach		Do
John Roach		Do
Needham Roach	May 23 1797	Do
Angelina Roach	Dec. 19 1799	Do
Elizabeth Roach	Nov 6 1802	Do
Jas. P. Roach	Oct 18 1804	Do
Celia Roach	Oct 26 1806	Do
Joseph Roach	Jan. 9 1811	Do
Isaac J. Roach	Oct 13 1813	Do
Isaac Johnston		Baptizd
Weneford Johnston		Do

Marriages	Commencing	Deaths	Removals
Feb. 14. 1790	In Communion May 1817		
	Do		
	Do		Remov'd By Letter
	Do		
Apl 10 1819	Do		
	Do		
	Do		
	Do		Remov'd By Letter
	Do		
	Do		Do

Married	In Communion		
	Do	Apl 19. 1836	

21. Names	Births	Baptisms
James Law Elder	June 18 1766	Baptized
Rosannah Law	Sept. 29 1768	Do
Children		
Margaret C. Law	Jan. 15 1792	Do
Elizabeth Law	Oct. 15 1793	Do
Rachael Law	Oct. 7 1795	Do
Thos. J. Law	Nov. 30 1797	Do
John Law	Apl. 3 1800	Do
Jane C. Law	Oct. 15 1802	Do
Mary Law	Nov. 10 1806	Do
Jas. Porter Law	Oct. 23 1808	Do
Rosannah Law	July 14 1812	Do

Marriages	Communions	Deaths	Removals
March 17, 1791	In Communion		Remov'd by Letter
—	Do		Do
	Do		
—	Do		Do
—	Do		Do
—	Do		Do
—	Do		Do
—	Do		Do
—	Do		Do
—	Do		Do
—	Do		Do

22 Names	Births	Baptism
John Kirkpatrick {Elder}	Feb 14 1771	Baptized
Jane Kirkpatrick	Jan 20 1774	Do
John B Kirkpatrick {Children}		Do
Mary Kirkpatrick		Do
Thos Kirkpatrick		Do
Josiah Kirkpatrick	Aug 7 1798	Do
James Kirkpatrick	Jan 10 1800	Do
Jane M. Kirkpatrick	Novr 17 1801	Do
Alex. A. Kirkpatrick	Dec 11 1803	Do
Margaret Kirkpatrick	Novr 16 1805	Do
Aseneth Kirkpatrick	July 15 1807	Do
William B Kirkpatrick	Feby 5 1810	Do
Nancy E. Kirkpatrick	Aug 15 1813	Do

Marriages	Communions	Deaths	Removals
	In Communion		Remov'd By Letter
	Do		Do
	Do		Do
	Do		Do
	Do		Do
	Do		Do
	Do		Do

23 Names	Births	Baptisms
Ransom Gwyn		Baptized
Rebecca Gwyn		Baptized
= Children		
Mary Gwyn	Oct. 3. 1793	Do
Sarah Gwyn	Oct. 2 1796	Do
Hugh Gwyn	Sept. 25 1798	Do
Robert Gwyn	Nov. 18 1803	Do
Margaret Gwyn	Mar. 24 1809	Do
Elenor Gwyn	June 20. 1811	Do
Wm. Gwyn	Jan. 30 1815	Do
Rebecca Gwyn	Dec. 23 1819	Do

Marriages	Communions	Deaths	Removals
	In Communion	1848	Recd By Letter Recd By Letter
	Do 1848		
		Decr 1827	
	Do		
	Do		Removd by letter
	Do	Sept 26. 1840	
Nov. 13. 1842			Remd by letter

24. Names	Births	Baptism
Robert Smith	July 1758	Baptized
Margaret Smith	Mar. 4 1762	Do
= Children		
John Smith	May 25. 1784	Do
Rosannah Smith	Dec 6. 1786	Do
William Smith		Do
Rachael Smith	Sept. 21. 1892	Do
Jane Smith	Oct. 20. 1794	Do
Robert Smith	Nov. 19. 1796	Do
Hugh Smith	Oct. 12. 1798	Do
Saml. C. Smith	Nov. 17. 1801	Do
Jesse Smith	Jan. 3 1803	Do

Marriages	Communions	Deaths	Removals
1791	In Communion Jan 21. 1823		
	Do	Nov. 2. 1835	
	Do		Remov'd by Letter Oct. 11. 1822
	Do		
	Do	died Sept. 1846	
	Do		
	Do	Sept. 26. 1818	
	Do	Apl. 23. 1823	
	Do	Octr. 1846	

25. Names	Births	Baptisms
Thos. Telford Elder	Novr. 11, 1786	Baptizd
Elizabeth Telford	May 13 1783	Do
Children		
Hugh Telford	Septr. 29. 1809	Do
Nancy Telford	Apl. 15. 1811	Do
Jane Telford	Apl. 14. 1813	Do
Esther K. Telford	Apl. 7. 1815	Do
Maryan F. Telford	twin	Do
Elizabeth S. Telford	Septr. 17. 1817	Do
Isabel C. Telford	Twin	
Margaret O. Telford	Janr. 29 1820	Mar. 26. 1820
Robert A Telford	Apl. 1 1822	Do
Rachael Telford	May 27. 1824	Do
Thos. H M Telford	Janr. 6 1827	Feb. 26. 1827

Marriages	Communions	Deaths	Removals
No 20 1808	In Communion	Mar. 2nd 1857	March 2nd
	Do	Jan. 16. 1842	

Thomas Jeffore expelled Religion 1811
at Old Ridge Meeting house

18 Do
24 × 23
Do
Do   Excluded
Do
                        1820
                        1822
                    Oct. 1817
Do

26 Names	Bairths	Baptisms
Samuel Brown		Baptized
Elizabeth Brown		Do
Children		
Ja: M. Brown	Apl. 14 1803	Do
Robert Brown {twin	May 26. 1807	Do
Margaret Brown}	May 26. 1807	Do
Elizabeth Brown	Decr 3. 1809	Do
Rosannah Brown	Decr 7 1811	Do
John S Brown	Apl. 27 1815	Do
William Brown	Apl. 14 1819	Do
Samuel Brown (Second Marriage)		Do
Nancy Brown		Do
Children		
Samuel Houston Brown	Sept 9 1835	Do

Marriages	Communions	Deaths	Removals
Mar. 26, 1801	In Communion Sept. 6, 1840		
	Do Aug 7, 1833		
	Do		
	Do		
	Do		Remov by letter
	Do		
	Do		
	Do		
Oct. 30, 1834	Do		

27 Names	Births	Baptisms
John Currey	Apr. 30 1762	Baptized
Sarah Currey	Sept. 10 1766	Do
Children		
Isaiah Currey	July 8 1788	Do
Jane Currey	Apr. 12 1790	Do
Elijah Currey	July 10 1792	Do
Susannah B. Currey	Oct. 15 1795	Do
Abner B Currey	Dec. 1 1797	Do
Elizabeth Currey	Nov. 15 1801	Do
Sarah H. Currey	Dec. 26 1804	Do
Margaret C. Currey	Nov. 5 1807	Do

Marriages	Communions	Deaths	Removals
July 29, 1784	In communion	Sept. 5. 1840	
	Do	Oct. 30. 1843	
	Do		
	Do		Remov'd By Letter
	Do		Do
	Do		
	Do		Remov'd By Letter
	Do		Do 1847

28

Names	Births	Baptisms
John Hamilton	May 30 1769	Baptized
Mary Hamilton		
Children		
Margaret Hamilton	Decr 1 1801	Do
Hannah K. Hamilton	Aug 2 1803	Do
Mary Hamilton	Mar. 6 1805	Do
George G. Hamilton	Aprl 23. 1808	Do

Jas. Bradford	Sept 29. 1775	Baptized
Elizabeth Bradford	Feb. 13 1783	Do
Eli. M. Bradford	Aug 30 1804	Do
Malinda D Bradford	Mar. 31. 1806	Do
Wm. M. Bradford	July 13. 1807	Do

Marriages	Communion	Deaths	Removals
	In Communion		Remo'd by Letter

July 2. 1803	In Communion	1848	
	Do	1876. aged 73 yrs	
		July 26. 1838	
			July 24. 1831

29.	Names	Bairths	Baptisms
John Rea		Baptized
Anna Rea		Do

Children

Jas. W. Rea	Jan. 6. 1805	Do
Margaret Rea	Feb. 23. 1807	Do
Wm. Rea	Apl. 20. 1809	Do
John Rea	May 5. 1811	Do
Isbel Rea	May 21. 1814	Do
Elizabeth Ann Rea	July 9. 1817	Do
Josiah I. Rea	Dr 2. 1819	Do
Samuel Rea	Nor. 22. 1822	Do
Mary Jane Rea	Feb. 27. 1826	Do

Marriages	Communions	Deaths	Removals
Mar. 1804	In Communion		
	Do	Died 1848	
Sept 18. 1830	Do		
	Do		Remov'd by Letter
	Do	Oct. 22. 1836	
	Do		
	Do	Mar. 3. 1834	
	Do	Mar. 7. 1834	
		Mar. 5. 1834	
		June 11. 1824	
	Do		

30 Names	Births	Baptisms
Reuben Wood Elder	Oct 10. 1787	Baptized
Jane Wood	Apl 12. 1790	Do
Children		
John C Wood	June 7. 1812	Do
Susannah M Wood	De 8. 1813	Do
David F Wood	Mar 11. 1816	Do
Reuben M Wood	Oct 3. 1817	Do
Jane H Wood	De 28. 1820	Do
Isaiah B Wood	Mar 10. 1824	Do

Marriages	Communions	Deaths	Removals
No. 13 1810	In Communion Sept. 9, 1835		
	Do Sept 28th 1846		
Sept 21, 1831			
	Do		
	Do May 29 1845		
	Do		
	Do		
	Do	July 7 1840	

31 Names	Births	Baptisms
John Roach Elder	Jan 23. 1794	Baptized
Mary Roach	Jan. 13. 1792	Do
Children		
John H. Roach	May 15. 1816	Do
Thos. K. Roach	Oct 13. 1817	Do
Alex. A. F. Roach	Sept 18. 1819	Do
Angelina M. Roach	May 1. 1821	Do
Jas. P. Roach	Feb. 17 1823	Do
Loiza Jane Roach	Jan. 7 1825	Do
Racheel E Roach	Jan. 1 1828	Do
Emuline Roach		
E. C. Roach		

Marriages	Communicants	Deaths	Removals
Aug 24, 1815	In Communion		By letter 1848
	Do		Do Do
	Do		
	Do		{ Remov'd by letter / Rec'd by Do }
	Do		Remov by letter
	Jan 2, 1822		
	Do		By letter 1848
	Do		Do Do
	Do		Do Do
	Do		Do Do
	Do		Do Do

32 Names	Births	Baptisms
Wm Roach	Feb 23 1791	Baptized
Anna Roach	1791	Do
Children		
Rachael H Roach	Apr 15 1816	Do
Mary S Roach	Nov 27 1817	Do
Elizabeth Ann Roach	Feb 7 1820	Do
Nancy A Roach	May 28 1822	Do
Angelina C Roach	July 10 1824	Do
Elenor P Roach	Mar 1 1827	Do
John H Roach	Aug 16 1829	Do
Celia B Roach	May 1 1832	Do

Marriages	Communicants	Deaths	Removals
Sept 15 - 1814	In Communion		Remov'd by Letter
	Do		Do

33 Names	Births	Baptisms
Elijah Currey Elder	July 10. 1792	Baptized
Margaret C Currey	Jan 15. 1792	Do
Wm Telford	June 8. 1777	Baptized
Elizabeth Telford	Oct 15. 1778	Do
Children		
Samuel W Telford	Jan 29 1803	Do
Mary Telford	Oct 8. 1804	Do
Elizabeth S Telford	Jan 22 1807	Do
Thos E Telford	Oct 31 1808	Do
John Telford	July 27 1810	Do
Ann Telford	Aug 14 1812	Do
Wm W Telford	Feb 19 1815	Do
Louiza Telford	Mar 5 1819	Do

Marriages	Communions	Deaths	Removals
	July 20. 1813 In Communion		1845 Removed by letter
	Do		Do
Ap 1802	Do		Removed by Letter
	Do		Do
	Do		
	Do		

Names	Births	Baptisms
John Telford	Oct. 1st 1790	Baptized
Sarah Telford	July 3 1786	Do
Children		
Hugh Telford		Do
Mary Telford		Mar 26, 1821
Elizabeth Ann Telford		Do
Andrew J. Telford		Do
Wm. G. Telford		Do
Hugh A. Telford	Oct 2 1798	Baptized
Mary W. Telford		Do
Children		
Elizabeth Ann Telford		

Marriages	Communions	Deaths	Removals
Nov 20, 1817	In Communion		Removed By Letter
	Do		Do
	Do		Do
	In Communion	1842	
	Do		
	do		

35 | Names | Births | Baptisms

David Bradford Aug 1 1778 — Baptized
Mary Bradford Oct 7 1787 — Do
— Children
Susannah Bradford Oct 24 1804 — Do
Samuel C. H. Bradford July 24 1808 — Do
Mary Ann Bradford June 30 1811 — Do
Sarah M. Bradford Feb 13 1814 — Do

Josiah Kirkpatrick Aug 7 1798 — Baptized
Nancy Kirkpatrick Ap 7 1791 — Do
— Children
Robert Kirkpatrick — Do
Sarah Kirkpatrick Jan 17 1820 — Do

Marriages	Communions	Deaths	Removals
1803 1803	In Communion		Remov'd by Letter
	Do		Do

Ap. 1819	In Communion		Remov'd by Letter
	Do		Do

36. Names	Births	Baptisms
Aaron Sprouse	Mar 8 1771	Baptized
Elizabeth Sprouse		Do
Children		
John G. Sprouse	Aug 21 1801	Do
Margaret C Sprouse	Sept 7 1803	Do
Nancy Sprouse	Oct 8 1805	Do
Rachael Sprouse	Nov 3 1807	Do
Mary Sprouse	Dec 11 1810	Do
George D Sprouse	Apr 24 1815	Do
Wm Sprouse	July 19 1817	Do
Joseph H Roach	Jan 9 1811	Baptized
Mary D Roach		Do
Children		
John Beard		Baptized

Marriages	Communions	Deaths	Removals
Dec 31, 1799			
	In communion		Received by letter
	Aug 16, 1820		Do
	Do		Do
	Do		Do
	1821		
	1823		
	1824		
Dec 1, 1830	In communion		
	Do		

37 Names   Births   Baptisms
Jas Yandle   Baptized
Mary Yandle   Do
    Children
John Yandle   Oct 16 1805   Do
Catharine Yandle   Aug 31 1807   Do
Wm. Yandle   Aug 31 1809   Do
Thos K. Yandle   Aug 6 1811   Do
Polley Ann Yandle   Sept 15 1813   Do
Jas. H. Yandle   July 2 1815   Do

Wm Smith   Baptized
Elizabeth Smith   Do
    Children
Jeeson Smith   Novr 24 1816   Do
Margaret Smith   Do

Marriages	Communions	Deaths	Removals
	In communion	Died	
	Do	Died	
	Do		
	Do		
	Do		Dismissed by consent
	Do		
	Do		
	Do		
	In communion July 5, 1819		
	Do		

38 Names	Births	Baptisms
Andrew Gwyn	Oct 13 1800	Baptized
Esther Gwyn		Do
Children		
Hugh R Gwyn		Feb 23 1823
Ransom R Gwyn		Mar 27 1825
Fax R Gwyn		Do
Elizabeth E Gwyn		1848 Do
Esther R Gwyn		do do
Rebecca M Gwyn		do

Marriages	Communions	Deaths	Removals
	Aug 30 1821 In communion		
	Do		
	Do		Removd by Letter
	Do		Removd by Letter
	Do		Withdrawn
	Do		
	Do		
	Do		

39 | Names | Births | Baptisms
Jesse Smith | Jan 3 1803 | Baptized
Latty Smith | | Do
Children
John S Smith | | Jan 1827
Margaret J Smith | | Do
Robert Monroe Smith | | Do

Marriages Communions Deaths Removals

In communion Oct. 1818
Do Apl. 22. 1840

Names	Births	Baptisms
40		
Nancy Currey (Widow)	—	Baptiz
Children		
John B Currey		Do
Robert B Currey		Do
James H Currey		Do
Ezekiel S Currey	Nov 1800	Do
Lane S Currey		Do
Lavina B Currey		Do
Elizabeth Currey		Do
Isaac N Currey	June 8. 1809	Do
Moses M Currey	Nov 23. 1811	Do

Marriages	Communions	Deaths	Removals
	In communion		
	Do	Feb. 18. 1833	
	Do	1815	
	Do	Augst 6th 1840	
	Do		

41 Names	Births	Baptisms
Owen Quinley		Baptizd
Mary Quinley		do
Children		
Mary Ann Quinley		do
Wm C Quinley		do
David M Quinley		do
John C Quinley		do
Nancy E Quinley		do

Marriages Communions Deaths Removals

In Communion

Do

Do
Do

42 Names	Births	Baptisms
Robert Brown	May 26 1807	Baptiz'd
Mary Brown	Aug 10th 1808	Do
Children Names		
Elizabeth J Brown	June 26 1828	Do
Nancy Aann Brown	Sept 22 1829	Do
Ira E Brown	Mar 11 1832	
Margaret R Brown	Apr 27 1835	

Marriages	Communions	Deaths	Removals
Married Aug 10th 1827	in Communion		
"	Do Augst 3rd 1846		
	Do		
	Do		
	Do 1845		

43

Names	Births	Baptisms
Needham Roach	May 23 1777	Baptiz'd
Fanney Roach	Decm 25 1777	Do
Children		
Sarah H Roach	Jan 30 1820	Do
Evaline L Roach	Apl 20 1822	Do
Rachael E Roach		Do
John H Roach		Do
Josiah E Roach		Do
James M Brown	Apl 14 1803	Baptiz'd
Celia Brown	Oct 26 1806	Do

Marriages	Communions	Deaths	Removals
10/10 1819	In Communion		Removed
"	Do		By Letter

Married			
"	In communion		

44

Names	Births	Baptisms
James Drennan Esqr	Sept 8 1787	Baptizd
Francis Drennan	June 13 1787	Do

Children

John Drennan	Mar 2 1810	Do
Joseph A Drennan	Dec 2 1811	Do
Sarah W Drennan	Oct 4 1814	Do
Catharine A Drennan	Octr 10 1816	Do
Eliza J Drennan	Sept 15 1818	Do
Wm B Drennan	Octr 30 1820	Do
Rebeca A Drennan	Dec 6 1822	Jar 27 182
Jas A Drennan	May 20 1825	June 24 182
Rachael A. J. Drennan	May 5 1827	July 24 18
Thos J Drennan	June 27 1829	Do
Andrew J Drennan	Do Do Do	Do

Marriages	Communions	Deaths	Removals
June 22 1809	In Communion		Removd By letter of Dismission
"	Do	1836	Receivd By letter
Aug 1830	Do		Removd by letter
	Do		Do
Sept 21 1831	Do		Do
	Do		Do
	Do		Do
		19 Feb. 1840	
	Do		Do By letter
18 Do 1842			Dec 25 1857
	Do		
	Do Do		

45

Names	Births (1798)	Baptisms
Hugh Smith	Oct 12 1898	Baptiz'd
Elizabeth Smith	Nov. 6. 1802	Do
Children		
Rachael R. Smith	Apl. 2 1822	Do
Celia L. Smith	Jan. 19 1824	Do
Margaret A Smith		Do

Marriages	Communions	Deaths	Removals
Married	In Communion		Removed by Letter
"	Do		Do

46

Names	Births	Baptisms
Wm Brown		Baptiz.^d
Jane Brown		Do
Children		
Sarah C Brown		Do
Margaret Brown		Do
Ann B Brown		Do
Rachael C Brown		Do
Ross Brown		Do
Hugh Brown		Do
Elizabeth C Brown		Do

Marriages	Communions	Deaths	Removals
	In Communion		
	Do		
	Do		
	Do		
	Do		
	Do	1840	
	Do		

47 Names   Births   Baptisms
Matt H Hooker   Baptiz
Nancy B Hooker   Do
        Children
Mary L Hooker   Do
Martha C Hooker

———————————————————————

Ezekiel S Currey   No   1800   Do
Rebecca Currey   Do

Marriages	Communions	Deaths	Removals
Married	In Communion		By Letter
"	Do		Do
	Do		By Letter 1847
	Do		Do Do
			The above Rec'd by letter 1850

48 | Names | Births | Baptisms
Jacob Woodrum | | | Baptized

Benj. F. Woodrum | | | " Do

arriages	Communions	Deaths	Removals
ard	In Communion July 4. 1842		
	Do		Rem by letter 1851

49 | Names | Births | Baptisms
William Woodrum | aug 15 1814 | Baptized
Martha Woodrum | May 7 1819 |

Children

Frances A Woodrum | aug 17 1834 | Do
Colantha Jane Woodrum | Dec 17 1836 | Do

Marriages	Communions	Deaths	Removals
Do	In Communion July 4 1847		Removed by letter
July 30 1829	Do		Do Oct 25
			Do 1837
	Do Do		Do
	Do Do		Do

45ᵃ Names	Births	Baptisms
Alison Posey		Baptiz

Reubem A. Wood	Oct 3 1817	do
Hester A Wood	August 23, 1821	do
Children		
Thoˢ. Lunsford. Wood	Febʳ 14ᵗʰ 1841	
Reuben. Mariette. Wood	May 4 1843	
Elizabeth L. A — Wood	September 9 1845	
Martha Jane Taylor Wood	January 8. 1848	

Marriages	Communions	Deaths	Removals
ied	In Communion		
July 30th 1839	Do		Removed by letter
	Do		Do
		Decr 13 1848	

57 Names	Births	Baptism
Thomas Glisson		Baptizd
Sarah Glisson		Do
Plesent A. Markham		Do
Jane Markham		Do

rriages	Communicant	Deaths	Removals
ued	In Communion		absconded
"	Do	1846	
	Do	Oct 18 1844	
	Do		

52

Names	Births	Baptism
Hugh Brown	4 Dec. 1815	Baptiz
Lamiza Brown	Apl 16	Do
Children		
James M. Brown	Mar 2, 1837	Do
Elizabeth A. Brown	May 4 1839	aug 18. 1839
William C. Brown Born Aug 22, 1841		
William C. Brown died Nov 6 19.13		

...riage	Communion	Deaths	Removals
...d Aug 20 1835	Do		Remov'd by Letter
"	Do		Remov'd by do 1847
			Do
			the above Rec'd By letter

Names	Births	Baptism
Ross Brown		Bapt⁻
Rosannah Brown	Dec⁻ 7 1811	do

rriages. Communions. Deaths. Removals

19th 1835 — In comunion

In Communion

54

Names	Births	Baptisms
David J. Wood	Mar. 11. 1816	Baptized
Ann B. Wood	June 18. 1814	Do
Children		
Sarah J Wood	Mar. 14. 1836	Aug 24 18_
Susannah A. Wood	Jan. 4 1838	July 8. 18_

ages	Communions	Deaths	Removals
7/7.1835	Do	May 29th 1845	
	In communion		
	Do. 1848		
		May 23, 1848	

55

Names	Births	Baptism
John C Wood	June 7 1812	Baptizd
Sarah W. Wood	Dec 4 1814	Do
Jas. D. Wood		
S. C. Wood		
I. B. Wood		
C. A. Wood		

Marriages	Communion	Deaths	Removals
Feb 21 1831			
"	In Communion	—	Removed By Letter

Names	Births	Baptisms
Matt. Whitaker		Baptiz'd
Nancy Whitaker		Do
& Children		
Mary Whitaker		Do
Martha Whitaker		Do
Moses M. Currey	Mar 23. 1811	Do
Margaret Currey	Dec 31 1807	Do

| Marriages | Communicants | Deaths | Memorials |

2nd In Communion
"   Do

in communion
Do

Names	Births	Baptisms
Thomas E. Roach	Oct 13 1817	Baptized
Nancy W. Roach	Sept 4 1817	Do
Children		
L. C. Roach		Do

arriages	Communement	Deaths	Removals
	July 16. 1835. In Communion		Removed by letter
"	Do		Recd by Do
			Removed by letter
	Do	1840	Do
	Do		
	Do 1845		Do

Names	Births	Baptisms
Isaac G. Barr		
Caroline Barr		

Hugh Telford Minister Sept 29 1809 Baptised

Julia A. B. Telford Born Feb 1. 1819

Children

Wm. Thos. A. Telford Sept 5 1843 Baptised
Samuel R. Brown Telford Jan.y 13 1845 Baptised

Richard Beard Telford Mar. 9, 1847
Rebecca E. B. Telford June 27, 1850
Hugh B. Hill Telford Aug. 31, 1852
Andrew F. Telford Sept 22, 1855

rinyees	Communions	Deaths	Removals
	In communion		
	Do		1844

April 20, 1842 In communion

Died
Aug. 29. 1855

Names	Births	Baptism
James Bradford Jr.		do
Rachel Bradford		do

Marriages   Communions   Deaths   Removals
              Do   Parish Registers
              Do   Do

	Births	Baptisms
Robert Foster, Elder	July 4" 1807	Baptized
Margaret Foster	February 23 1787	Do
Children		
Wm Foster	July 9th 1828	Do
Ann J Foster	~~ 10 1831	Do
Isabel R. Foster	January 7 1834	Do
James D Foster	June 12, 1836	Do
John Foster	January 8 1839	Do
Andrew J Foster	Aprile 24. 1841	Do
Robert Foster	July 4 1807	Do
Second Marriage		
Nancy Foster	October 29. 1810	Do
Children		
Robert C. Foster	June 17 1847	Do

Carriages	Communions	Deaths	Removals
	In Communion		
	Do		
	Do	January 9, 1844	
	Do	May 19 1851	
		October 1, 1840	
	Do		
December 24 1845			
	Do		

Names of Individuals	Births	Baptisms
Henry Devault		"
James Robbins		"
Elmira A. Robins		"
Elizabeth Barr		"
Malinda Carter		"
William M'Ginness		
Tennessee Randall		
John B. Kirkpatrick		
Hamen M. Robbins		
James Parum		
Hugh R. Gwynn		
Morris Gooden		
Rachael Drennan		
Rachael Telford		
Elizabeth A. Telford		
Rhoda Ann Ford		
Delanta Ann Robbins		

Communions	Deaths	Removals
Do		Remov[d by letter]
Do		Remov[d by letter]
Do	Died Agst 27. 1844	
Do	Dead	
Do		Remov'd by letter
Do	Died 1844	
Do	Dead 1848	Removed [by letter]
Do		
Do	Died 1846	
Do		Removed
Do		Remov by Letter
Do		Remov
Do		Remov by letter
Do		
Do		
Do		Remov

Names of Individuals. Births	Baptized
Priscilla Finney	Baptized
Mrs Patsy Dobson	Do
William Shice	Do
Mary Wright	Do
Elizabeth E. Osborn	Aug 21. 1836
Hester A Osborn	" 21 1836
Margaret O Telford	" Do
Hubbard Cawthon	Aug 23 183
Wm Cawthon	" 23 183
Bennetta Brown	
Sally Ward	Do
Sally Davis	Do
Jane Davis	Do
Cintha Davis	Do
Stephen Woodrum	Do
Polley Ford	

In communion   Death   Removal
In communion
       Do
       Do   Removed by letter 1843
       Do
       Do
       Do
       Do
       Do
       Do

       Do   Sept 26. 1839
       Do   Jan 18. 1843
       Do
1834   Do
       Do   Dismissed Jan 1 1839
       Do   by consent

Names of Individuals	Births	Baptisms
B. C. Brown		Baptiz'd
Lucinda Beard		Do
Rebecca McDaniel		Do
Susannah Hamilton		Do
Delilah Welch		Do
Tabitha Aheart		Do
Mitchel Welch		Do
Ezekiel S. Currey		Do
Mary E. Hamilton		Do
Mrs Ann Chandler		Do
Nancy Smith		Do
Robert A. Finney		Do
Martha Woodrum		Do
Tabitha J. Woodrum		Do
Demaris Parum		Do
Mrs Margaret Hooker		Do

Communicants	Deaths	Removals
In Communion		Remov'd by letter
Do		Remov'd by letter Oct 26
Do		
Do		Remov'd by letter
Do	Died	
Do		in disorder
Do		
Do		
Do		Remov'd by letter
Do		Remov'd by letter
Do	Died — 1840	
Do		Remov'd by letter
Do		Remov'd by letter Jan 2 1842
Do		
Do		
Do		

Names of Individuals	Births	Baptisms
J. Jacobs	—	Baptised
Nancy Brown		Do
Caroline Huddleson		Do
Burril P. Smith	—	Aug 15. 1841
Robert Climer		Do
Hugh Kelsey Bell		
Samuel Hanveltton		
Ira P. Davis		
John H. Bush		
Rachael Roach		
Lunetta Glessen		
Jane Cunningham	— — —	Aug 15. 1841
Lucinda H Cawthon		
Susannah F Cawthon		
Isaac N. Cawthon		Aug 14 1842
Mary an Huddleston		Do
Jas. A. Drennan		
Alfred Vernum		
William Morgan		

Marriages	Communions in communion	Deaths	Removals
	Do		Removd by letter
	Do	Died 1844	
	Aug 15 1841		Removd by letter
	Do		
	Do		Removd by letter Oct 15, 1841
	Do		
	Do	Feby 27th 1846	
	Do		
	Do		
	Do		Removd by letter
	Do		
	Dec 25		Recv by letter
	" 25		Removd by letter
	Do		
	Do		
	Do		
	Do		
	Do		in disorder

Names Individuals	Births	Baptism
Eda Rea		Baptised
Malinda Sullivan		Do Do
John B Jackson		Do Do
Elizabeth Dobson		Do
Houston Caulthon		Do
Emeline Roach		Do
Thos. J. Drennan		Do
Elizabeth Jackson		Do
Minerva Jackson		Do
Malinda Barefoot		Do
Ann Foster		Do
Isabel Foster		Do
W. S. Woodrum		Do
Jas. N. Yandell		Do
E. C. Roach		Do
H. C. Bonner		Do
F. B. Jackson		

Mariages	Communion	Deaths	Removals
	In Communion Died	1846	
	Do		
	Do Do		
	Do Do		
	Do Do	—	Removd by Lett.
	Do Do	—	Removd by letter
	Do Do		
	Do Do		
	Do Do		
	Do Do	Died 1849	
	Do Do	Died 1845	
	Do Do		
	Do		
	Do		
	Do	—	Removd by letter
	Do 1848		
	Do Do		

	Births	Bapt.
L. D. Jackson		do
Caroline Dobson		do
Sarah W[illiam?]son		do
Susan M. Barr		do
Sarah E. Carter		do
Christian Sublett		do
Liliana Barr		do
Will S. Kirkpatrick		do
L. E. C. Kirkpatrick		do
Susan Eackles		do
Nancy Jackson		do
Mary R. Carter		do
Elizabeth Harrison		"
Sophona Gwyn		"
William Brown		"
Monroe Smith		1850
Edw Eackles		
Wm Jackrey		
Margaret Smith		

Marriages Banns   Births   Burials
            Do   1848
            Do   Do
            Do   Do   1842
            Do   Do
            Do   Do
            Do   Do   Removed by
            Do   Do   a letter
            Do   Do
            Do   Do
            Do   Do   do
            Do

Church 1870 births | Bapt

G. McMinn | baptized
Margaret Brown | do
Jas B Dobson | do
Thankful Griffin | do
Ely Griffin | do
S J Griffin | do
A E Dobson | do
Elisa Dobson | do
Amanda Cotton | do
Julya Winters | do
S J Yandell | do
R J Kirkpatrick | do
S A Kirkpatrick | do
Margaret Sneith | do
Bedford Rice | do
Ross Brown | do
Nancy Dobson | do
Jane Bearfield |

Name	B...	Bapt
Robt W Hooker	" "	" "
Isaack M Cottrem	" "	" "
Rachel E Cottrem	" "	" "
Obey Kirkpatrick		
Joseph Smith		Baptized
Thena Rice		Do
Messianna Rice		Do
Elisabeth Marison		Do
Miriam Hugle		Do
Elizabeth Woodrum		Do
Clem Rice		Do
Martha Rice		Do
Ruth J. Rollins		Do
William Mines		Do
Sarah Ann Dolson		Do
Ester J. Dolson		

116

mary bean   tract   [illegible]
  " "   By letter
  " "   By letter
  " "   By lett
  " "   By lett
                            By lett
      do
      do

      Do
      Do   Removed by
                            letter 1854
      Do
      Do
      Do
      Do
      Do
      Do
      Do

Names	Births	Bapt.
Eveline Mines		Do
Lucy Jones		Do
~~		Do
Sarah A Wiley		
Jackson		
Jackson		
Amanda Walker's Servant		Baptized
Minna Sherel		
Martha June Devault	Received	
Cordelia Ann Mines		
Rachel Elizabeth Wood	Aug 17	Adult
Sarah Elizabeth Telford		
Wm T. R. Telford		
Reb: Ann Cory	1	

Marriage	Commun.	Deaths	Remov.
1852	Do		
	Do		
	Do		Remov'd by letter Feb 23. 1854

July 57 Do

April 857 1858

Octo 1858

Birth | Death

John B. Shields — Richard C. Phillips
was born Sep 15, 1844 Sep 22, 1911

W. E. Fields departed from this life
Aug 17, 1914

J. E. Sanders was born June 12, 1839
Willie E Sanders was born July 3, 1877
Berthum Sanders was born Dec 5, 1905

this Aug 27, 1914

E. A. Lannom was Married to
Belle Bilbro   Feb 1   1893

E. A. Lannom   Was Born July 23 1867

Belle Lannom   Was Born Ap 3 1871

Children

E. O. Lannom   Was B Dec 23 1893

M. E. Lannom   " Feb 20 1896

Eva A Lannom   " Nov 15 1898

Ruly B Lannom   " Nov 3 1900

Alma J Lannom   " July 3 1903

Martin D Lannom " Dec 9 1905

Little Nell Lannom B Feb 1 1912

Ruth Lucile Lannom B Aug 9 1915

Marriage Record.

Omer Estle Lannom was married
to Thelma Beatrice Griffin
　　Sunday, July 11, 1920.

James Wilson Knight was married
to Alma Jane Lannom
　　Thursday, November 26, 1925.

Martin Douglas Lannom was married
to Annie Lucile Carlow
　　Sunday, April 15, 1928.

Robert Mack Davenport was married
to Mary Elizabeth Lannom
　　Sunday, October 14, 1928.

Melvin Vincent Andrews Jr. was married
to Ruth Lucile Lannom
　　Thursday April 23, 1936.

"Grandchildren" Births.

Omer E. Lannom, Jr., born Tuesday August 5, 1924.
Patricia Griffin Lannom, born Monday November 28, 1927.
Barbara Jo Lannom, born Wednesday November 16, 1932.

Joyce Wilarlie Knight, born Thursday February 17, 1927
Kenneth Lannom Knight, born Thursday July 16, 1931

William Douglas Lannom, born Friday March 8, 1929
Donald Ray Lannom, born Wednesday May 17, 1933

Robert Bilbo Andrews born Saturday July 19, 1941.
Carl Jean Andrews born Sat. April 13, 1946.

123

Thelma Beatrice Griffin — born
February 18, 1901

James Wilcox Knight — born
June 5, 1896

Robert Mack Davenport — born
Oct. 5, 1880

Annie Lucile Carloss — born
March 28, 1907

Melvin Vincent Andrews — born
January 21st, 1915

Deaths

E. A. Lammers died on or about the 28 of July - 1945.

Bill Bithot Lammers died August 11, 1930 mm

Omer E. Lammers died May 2, 1963 shure

James Wilson Knight died May 6, 1961 3rd

Little Nell Lammers died Feb. 8, 1914

Eva Allen Lammers died Dec. 26, 1917.

Robert Mack Davenport died Feb. 17, 1959 Tues.

Grand children of
Jamie Wilson Knight and Alma L.
Knight.

Linda Faye Knight born Fri Oct. 23, 1953.
Kenneth L. Knight Jr. born Thurs. Nov. 4, 1954
Ronald Wayne Knight born Sat. Sept. 13, 1958
Karen Lee Knight born Fri. Sept. 23, 1960
David Alan Knight born Thurs. July 12, 1962

Rebecca Jane Bails born mon. July 11, 1955
Deborah Ruth Bails born Tues. March 3, 1959
~~Robert Mick Davenport~~

NAME INDEX

Aheart, Tabitha 106
Anderson, Alexander 4
Andrews, Carloss J. 123
Andrews, Melvin V. 122,124
Andrews, Robert B. 123
Arnold, John 11
Baito, Deborah J. 126
Baito, Rebecca J. 126
Barber, Thomas J. 11
Barefoot, Malinda 110
Barr, Caroline 96
Barr, Chana 112
Barr, Elizabeth 102
Barr, Isaac G. 96
Barr, Susan 112
Beard, John 4,7,10,52
Beard, Lucinda 106
Bearfoot, Jane 114
Bell, Hugh 108
Bilbro, Bell 121
Binkly, Henry J. 7
Bonner, H. C. 110
Bradford, David 50
Bradford, Eli M. 7,36
Bradford, Elizabeth 36
Bradford, James 36,98
Bradford, Malinda D. 36
Bradford, Mary 50
Bradford, Rachael 98
Bradford, Samuel C. 50
Bradford, Sarah W. 50
Bradford, Susannah 50
Bradford, William M. 36
Brown, Ann B. 72
Brown, B. C. 9,10,106
Brown, Celia 66
Brown, Elizabeth 32
Brown, Elizabeth A. 84
Brown, Elizabeth J. 64
Brown, Elizabeth L. 72
Brown, Hugh 72,84
Brown, Ira E. 64
Brown, James M. 32,66,84
Brown, Jane 72
Brown, John S. 32
Brown, L. 84
Brown, Margaret 32,72,114
Brown, Margaret R. 64
Brown, Mary 64
Brown, Nancy 32,108
Brown, Nancy A. 64
Brown, R. 5
Brown, Rachael C. 72

Brown, Robert 5,32,64
Brown, Rosannah 32,86
Brown, Ross 72,86,114
Brown, Samuel 32
Brown, Samuel H. 32
Brown, Sarah L. 72
Brown, William 32,72,112
Brown, William C. 84
Bush, John H. 108
Carloss, Annie L. 122,124
Carter, Malinda 102
Carter, Mary R. 112
Carter, Sarah 112
Carter, Solomon 7,8
Cawthan, J. N. 5
Cawthon, Hubbard 104
Cawthon, Huston 110
Cawthon, Isaac N. 108
Cawthon, J. H. 7
Cawthon, J. N. 5
Cawthon, John H. 7
Cawthon, Joseph 112
Cawthon, Lucinda H. 108
Cawthon, Susannah F. 108
Cawthon, William 104
Ceay, Reb A. 118
Chandler, Ann 106
Climer, Robert 108
Cothern, Amanda 112
Cothern, Rachel 116
Cothern, Sarah M. 116
Cunningham, Jane 108
Currey, Abner B. 34
Currey, E. 7
Currey, Elijah 7,8,9,11,34,46
Currey, Elizabeth 34,60
Currey, Ezekiel S. 60,74,106
Currey, Isaac N. 60
Currey, Isaiah 34
Currey, James H. 60
Currey, Jane 34
Currey, Jane S. 60
Currey, John 34
Currey, John B. 60
Currey, Lavina B. 60
Currey, M. M. 5,6
Currey, Margaret 34,92
Currey, Margaret C. 46
Currey, Moses M. 4,7,60,92
Currey, Nancy 60
Currey, Rebecca 74
Currey, Robert B. 60
Currey, Sarah 34

127

Currey, Sarah H. 34
Currey, Susannah B. 34
Curry, M. M. 5
Davenport, Robert M. 122, 124
Davis, Cintha 104
Davis, Ira P. 108
Davis, Jane 104
Davis, Sally 104
DeVault, Henry 102
DeVault, Martha J. 118
Dobson, A. E. 114
Dobson, Benjamin 18
Dobson, Caroline 112
Dobson, Elise 114
Dobson, Elizabeth 16,110
Dobson, Ester J. 116
Dobson, Jane 18
Dobson, Margaret 18
Dobson, Nancy 114
Dobson, Patsy 104
Dobson, Sarah A. 116
Dobson, Tho B. 114
Dobson, William R. 18
Donnel, Samuel 4
Drennan, Andrew J. 68
Drennan, Ann 11
Drennan, Catherine A. 68
Drennan, David 11
Drennan, Eliza 68
Drennan, Frances 68
Drennan, James 4,11,68
Drennan, James A. 68,108
Drennan, John 11,68
Drennan, Joseph 11
Drennan, Joseph A. 68
Drennan, Rachael 102
Drennan, Rachael A. 68
Drennan, Rachel 11
Drennan, Rebecca A. 68
Drennan, Sarah W. 68
Drennan, Thomas J. 68,110
Drennan, Thomas S. 11
Drennan, William 11
Drennan, William B. 68
Eakes, Edward 112
Fields, John B. 120
Fields, W. E. 120
Finney, Robert A. 106
Ford, Polly 104
Ford, Rhoda A. 102
Foster, Andrew J. 100
Foster, Ann 12,100,110
Foster, David 4,6,12

Foster, Elizabeth A. 12
Foster, Isabel 12,100,110
Foster, John 100
Foster, John C. 12
Foster, Margaret 100
Foster, Nancy 100
Foster, Nancy A. 12
Foster, R. 5
Foster, Robert 12,100
Foster, Robert E. 100
Foster, William 100
Foster, William C. 12
Glison, Lunetta 108
Glison, Sarah 82
Glison, Thomas 82
Gooden, Morris 102
Griffin, Ely 114
Griffin, L. J. 114
Griffin, Thankful 114
Griffin, Thelma B. 122,124
Gwyn, A. 7
Gwyn, Andrew 56
Gwyn, Elenor 26
Gwyn, Esther 56
Gwyn, Esther R. 56
Gwyn, Hugh 26
Gwyn, Hugh R. 56
Gwyn, James K. 56
Gwyn, Margaret 26
Gwyn, Mary 26
Gwyn, Ransom 26
Gwyn, Ransom R. 56
Gwyn, Rebecca M. 56
Gwyn, Robert 26
Gwyn, Sarah 26
Gwyn, Sophona 112
Gwyn, William 26
Gwynn, Hugh R. 102
Hamilton, George G. 36
Hamilton, John 36
Hamilton, Margaret 36
Hamilton, Mary 36
Hamilton, Mary E. 106
Hamilton, Samuel 108
Hamilton, Susannah 106
Hannah, John 4
Hannah, William 4
Harrison, Elizabeth 112
Hiers, M. 116
Hilton, Mr. 10
Hooker, Margaret 106
Hooker, Martha C. 74,92
Hooker, Mary 74,92
Hooker, Matt H. 74,92

Hooker, Nancy B. 74,92
Hooker, Robert W. 116
Huddleson, Caroline 108
Huddleston, Maryan 108
Hugle, Hirum 116
Jackson 118
Jackson, Elizabeth 110
Jackson, F. B. 110
Jackson, J. B. 4,5,6
Jackson, John B. 110
Jackson, L. D. 112
Jackson, Lissie 112
Jackson, Minerva 110
Jackson, Nancy 112
Jacobs, J. 108
Johnston, Isaac 20
Johnston, Wineford 20
Jones, Ignatius 18
Jones, Lucy 118
Jones, Mrs. 10
Jones, Needham 10
Jones, Wineford 18
King, Samuel 4
Kirkpatrick, Alex A. 24
Kirkpatrick, Aseneth 24
Kirkpatrick, James 24
Kirkpatrick, Jane 24
Kirkpatrick, Jane M. 24
Kirkpatrick, John 24
Kirkpatrick, John B. 102
Kirkpatrick, Josiah 24,50
Kirkpatrick, L. A. 114
Kirkpatrick, Margaret 24
Kirkpatrick, Mary 24
Kirkpatrick, Nancy 50
Kirkpatrick, Nancy E. 24
Kirkpatrick, Olley 116
Kirkpatrick, R. J. 114
Kirkpatrick, Robert 50
Kirkpatrick, S. E. 112
Kirkpatrick, Sarah 50
Kirkpatrick, Thomas 24
Kirkpatrick, Will 112
Kirkpatrick, William B. 24
Knight, Alma 126
Knight, David A. 126
Knight, James W. 122,124,125,126
Knight, Joyce W. 123
Knight, Karen L. 126
Knight, Kenneth L. 123,126
Knight, Linda F. 126
Knight, Ronald W. 126
Lackey, William 112

Lannom, Alma J. 121,122
Lannom, Barbara J. 123
Lannom, Belle 121
Lannom, Belle B. 125
Lannom, Donald R. 123
Lannom, E. A. 121,125
Lannom, Eva A. 121,124
Lannom, Little N. 124
Lannom, M. E. 121
Lannom, Martin 121
Lannom, Martin D. 122
Lannom, Mary E. 122
Lannom, Nell 121,124
Lannom, Omer E. 122,123,124
Lannom, Patrick G. 123
Lannom, Ruby B. 121
Lannom, Ruth L. 121,122
Lannom, William D. 123
Law, Elizabeth 22
Law, Gideon H. 4
Law, James 4,22
Law, James P. 22
Law, Jane C. 22
Law, John 22
Law, Margaret C. 22
Law, Mary 22
Law, Rachael 22
Law, Rosannah 22
Law, Thomas T. 22
Logue, Dr. 10
McDaniels, Rebecca 106
McDerman, Wilee 7
McDermon, Wilee 8
McGinnis, William 102
Markham, Plesent 82
Mier, G. W. 6
Miers, E. H. 6
Mires, Cordelia 118
Mires, Eveline 118
Mires, G. W. 114
Mires, William 116
Morgan, William 108
Morison, Elizabeth 116
Osborn, Dr. 10
Osborn, Elizabeth E. 104
Osborn, Hester A. 104
Osborn, T. C. 10
Osborn, Thomas 10
Partlow, Thomas 11
Parum, Demaris 106
Parum, James 102
Peach, G. 10
Posey, Allison 80
Provine, John 6

Puckett, Thomas A. 10
Quinley, David M. 62
Quinley, Haney E. 62
Quinley, John C. 62
Quinley, Mary 62
Quinley, Mary A. 62
Quinley, Owen 62
Quinley, William C. 62
Randall, Tennessee 102
Rea, Anna 38
Rea, Eda 110
Rea, Elizabeth A. 38
Rea, Isabel 38
Rea, James W. 38
Rea, John 38
Rea, Josiah T. 38
Rea, Mary J. 38
Rea, Samuel 38
Rea, William 38
Rice, Bedford 114
Rice, Betsy 6
Rice, Elem 116
Rice, Esther 6
Rice, Martha 116
Rice, Thena 116
Rice, William S. 104
Roach 8
Roach, Alex A. 42
Roach, Angelina 20
Roach, Angelina C. 44
Roach, Anna 44
Roach, Celia 20
Roach, Celia B. 44
Roach, E. C. 42,110
Roach, Elenor P. 44
Roach, Elizabeth 20
Roach, Elizabeth A. 44
Roach, Emeline 42
Roach, Eveline L. 66
Roach, Fanny 66
Roach, Harry W. 94
Roach, Isaac J. 20
Roach, J. J. 7
Roach, James P. 20,42
Roach, John 7,20,42,66
Roach, John B. 52
Roach, John F. 44
Roach, John N. 4,42
Roach, Joseph 20
Roach, Joseph H. 52
Roach, Josiah E. 66
Roach, L. C. 94
Roach, Louisa J. 42
Roach, Mary 42

Roach, Mary D. 52
Roach, Mary S. 44
Roach, Nancy A. 44
Roach, Needham 20,66
Roach, Rachael 20,108
Roach, Rachael E. 42,66
Roach, Sarah H. 66
Roach, Thomas 94
Roach, Thomas K. 42
Roach, William 20,44
Robbins, Delanta A. 102
Robbins, Flamen M. 102
Robbins, James 102
Robertson, Mary J. 11
Robins, Elmira A. 102
Rollins, Ruth J. 116
Rouch, Emeline 110
Sanders, Berthum 120
Sanders, J. E. 120
Sanders, Wille E. 120
Sherel, M. 118
Sinclair, Eli 7,8
Smith, Burrel P. 108
Smith, Elizabeth 54,70
Smith, Hugh 28,70
Smith, Iveson 54
Smith, Jane 28
Smith, Jesse 28,58
Smith, John 28
Smith, John S. 58
Smith, Joseph 116
Smith, Latty 58
Smith, Margaret 28,54,114
Smith, Margaret A. 70
Smith, Margaret J. 58
Smith, Monroe 112
Smith, Nancy 106
Smith, Rachael 28
Smith, Rachael R. 70
Smith, Robert 4,28
Smith, Robert M. 58
Smith, Rosannah 28
Smith, Samuel C. 28
Smith, William 28,54
Sprouse, Aaron 52
Sprouse, Elizabeth 52
Sprouse, George D. 52
Sprouse, John G. 52
Sprouse, Margaret C. 52
Sprouse, Mary 52
Sprouse, Nancy 52
Sprouse, Rachael 52
Sprouse, William 52
Sublett, Preston 112

Sullivan, Malinda 110
Telford, Andrew J. 48,96
Telford, Ann 14,46
Telford, Elizabeth 14,16,30,46
Telford, Elizabeth A. 48,102
Telford, Elizabeth S. 30,46
Telford, Esther H. 30
Telford, F. M. 6
Telford, H. 4,5,6,8
Telford, Hugh 4,6,14,16,30,48, 96
Telford, Hugh A. 14,48
Telford, Hugh B. 96
Telford, Isabel C. 30
Telford, Jane 14,16,30
Telford, John 14,46,48
Telford, Julia A. 96
Telford, L. E. 6
Telford, Louisa 46
Telford, M. F. 30
Telford, Margaret A. 104
Telford, Margaret O. 30
Telford, Mary 14,46,48
Telford, Mary W. 6,48
Telford, Nancy 16,30
Telford, Rachael 30,102
Telford, Rebecca E. 96
Telford, Richard B. 96
Telford, Robert 14,16
Telford, Robert A. 30
Telford, Samuel 16,96
Telford, Samuel K. 46
Telford, Sarah 16,48
Telford, Thomas 4,5,7,14,30
Telford, Thomas C. 16
Telford, Thomas E. 46
Telford, Thomas F. 30
Telford, Tirzah 16
Telford, Washington 16
Telford, William 46
Telford, William G. 48
Telford, William T. 96,118
Telford, William W. 46
Vernum, Alfred 108
Walker, Amanda 118
Ward, Sally 104
Welch, Delilah 106
Welch, Mitchel 106
Wiley, Sarah 118
Winters, Julia A. 6
Winters, Julya 114
Wood, Ann B. 88
Wood, David F. 40,88
Wood, Elizabeth L. 80

Wood, F. C. 90
Wood, Hester A. 80
Wood, Isaiah B. 40
Wood, J. B. 90
Wood, James D. 90
Wood, Jane 40
Wood, Jane H. 40
Wood, John C. 40,90
Wood, Martha J. 80
Wood, Rachael E. 118
Wood, Reuben 4,7,40
Wood, Reuben M. 4,40,80
Wood, Sarah J. 88
Wood, Sarah W. 90
Wood, Susannah A. 88
Wood, Susannah M. 40
Wood, Thomas L. 80
Woodrum, Benjamin F. 76
Woodrum, Colantha J. 78
Woodrum, Elizabeth 116
Woodrum, Frances 78
Woodrum, Jacob 76
Woodrum, Martha 78,106
Woodrum, Stephen 104
Woodrum, Tabitha 106
Woodrum, W. S. 110
Woodrum, William 4,78
Wright, Mary 104
Yandel, James S. 7,8
Yandell, James N. 110
Yandell, S. J. 114
Yandle, Catherine 54
Yandle, James 54
Yandle, James H. 54
Yandle, John 54
Yandle, Mary 54
Yandle, Polley A. 54
Yandle, Thomas K. 54
Yandle, William 7,8,54

www.ingramcontent.com/pod-product-compliance
Lightning Source LLC
LaVergne TN
LVHW090948310325
807311LV00008B/171